daisy
loft
content

by Daniel P. Padilla

gathering of sorts

Dantie Alighieri

Paradiso, XXX, vv. 97-120

O splendor of God! by means of which I
sow

The lofty triumph of the realm veracious,

Give me the power to say how I saw it!

There is a light above, which visible

Makes the Creator unto every creature,

Who only in beholding peace,

And it expands itself in circular form

To such extent, that its circumference

Would be too large a girdle for the sun.

The semblance of it is all made of rays

Reflected from the top of Primal Motion,

Which takes their form, vitality and power

And as a hill in water at its base

Mirrors itself, as if to see its beauty

When affluent most in verdure and in
flowers,

So ranged aloft all round about the lights

Mirrored I saw in more ranks than a
thousand

All who above there have from us returned

And if the lowest new collect within it

So great a light, how vast the amplitude

Is of these colors in its extremist leaves!

daisy loft content:

the Pro Tem

1. contents of film(stock)
                        noir/blanc

1 – distort

2 – frontier

3 – historic

4 – cave

5 – view

6 – scratches

7 – lean

8 – bright

9 – chafe

10 – petite

11- please

12 – foggy

13 – blurr

14 – blind

15 – dream

16 – spring

17 – logical

18 – mental

19 – wait

20 – space

memory

21– tap

22– dark

23– scan

2. Contents of the Apple Mysteries

Manifest series

(Atlantica as)

(forethought)

(is an arc of)

(boxes)

(floral)

(drupelets)

(girdling)

(orange)

(brighter purple lighter)

(grape harvest)

(rooting)

(alternately)

(green with the)

(artful)

(wax and)

(afterthought)

Found series

(Americano as)

(1)

(2)

(3)

(4)

Create series

(Continuum)

(introducing an apple's act as a)

(1) posthumous)
(2) revenge)
(3) surviving the red of)
(4) disappointment)
(5) stable and)
(6) toxic)
(7) capturing)
(8) bluish flesh)
(9) pleasing)
(10)   obtaining the)
(11)   completely)
(12)   guarded)

(concluding the apples are yellowish)

3. Contents of Waves to Curl

Waves 1-10

to 1-3

Curl 1-10

4. **Contents of Hamilton Street collection**

1 sand of (fabled) ports

1 - you

2 - I did not build this

3 - my own

4 — you find a moment

2 boom city busts

1 - so

2 - here

3 - we are

3 playlist for the flight

(I see you)

(Ok)

(I pass)

(and)

(wave to)

(the ground 35,000 feet below)

4 [eros 6 a.m.)

introduce — slabs of

1 - [I

2 — compose

3 – **to**

4 – **congeal)**

5 - **us**

conclude – we

5 sand of (fabled) ports continued

5 – (A) dust in the air

5 – (B) my Chest Full of Sand

6 – uncovery

7 - salt mine

6 salt

waking up

across town

lot

when hours pass

unloads a lunch break

5.   Contents of Orange's Codices

1

2

3

4

5

6. Contents of Wolves & Lions

1-24

7. contents: Rush the Light

oral tradition

Detroit

hacking a futurist from Marinetti's muscle car manifesto

Tesla's

fireworks

ex-pats

1. Bacon on the street
2. wild pictures on a gray day
3. Stoker's garden

back channel the moon

big grin

theatre from London

cowgirl up

outside in

500gm. cakes

Toulouse-Lautrec

I dreamt about Dali St. Petes and Chris in
Columbus cannibalizing my tears

Omaha, Normandy

sunflowers

clandestine in grey

old vine zen

1. color wheel (paints)
2. primary (strokes)
3. secondary (canvas)

bends (knots)

luchadores

missionary possible

tide

nonage

die a pause

combustible

phosphenes

cloud chamber

fireworks 2

henge

helios

Icarus' brew pub

roaring one

eight bank in the side

sawbones says

Julio Cortazar's "to be Read in the Interrogative" (to be read as a Jack Spicer imitation)

a Flight not All Ways

the Epitaph

the Pro Tem

is the extracting erasuresque
carving up the Sleeping Beauty by
Hayden Caruth for Thanksgiving
dinner (80-112) quotes.

Hell

Hath such fires, burning and

        consuming, themselves

Never consumed

Beauty is pain plus time

It's a kind of Unity, this heap.

        this undesigned

The dolmen is silent. It glows

Almost, thunderous almost in its

        sanctity of grief

But knowingly, drearily

Yet you only waltz'd and waltz'd

Word by word he forced his

        poems on his rigid

Tongue

If only one shred

Of consciousness remained

        one infinitesimal root

Of freedom, he swore he would save, to

Less red than deep blue, when

        clouds hide the yellow

Stylish and say and properly contorted

Ideas alone but anguish caught

In their living brains, a rational

relief;

His eyes are a deep green

Where hot lights pour down purple

vanishes orange

The exalting, reaching and

thrusting through lust

Insisting, commanding.

Our hills and fields, all the

shapes and colors

-you know their flashy

Way of talking

All proud and feisty-like, and

it makes on itch

You're grateful, but you don't

ever ask, you don't ever
talking

which ain't the whole of it
either

a field is

A speak of creation,

Cram-full of them that give

Up the geist

A bent figure in the dark

        thinly clothed

A pine staff in a mitten

        flashlight in the others

Slow-stepping from house to burn

Salt, coffee, a pack or two of

        Day's work,

The endless colorless weeping

        love like dropped

        mercury scattered

Mind is sleep

Dream, evolutionary error

        bound for extinction seen.

The star creep.

As if in blood on the well of

        consciousness

film(stock)
noir/blanc

sequenced prototypes of
mobile sonnets in the
spirit beyond form

distort   1

(filters)   noir/blanc

I like like the way

it looks looks

I don't like like the way

it feels peel

sticks in the creek

refract

needs to rinse in the muddy water under the

fluttering shade of an

oak tree's branches

sitting down into the

stream dream about

collages of old photographs

possessing several limbs and

poising beasts

frontier   2

(frames)   noir/blanc

there is nothing bigger in

this frontier

then the canyons

that gash into this

painted earth over the

centuries of droughts and

floods

cutting one way

one rock, one fish

one dinosaur

one tribe

one frame at a time

historic   3

(setting)   noir/blanc

I'm in this historic play
below the youth of the stars as
fresh and bold as dinosaurs' bones
puzzled together in a museum of
giant sloths
could not catch the
light of the meteors
just right to justify the
time it took to
brush away the grime of
long life underground a-
waiting to
be real again

cave   4

(print)   noir/blanc

who knows before?

we found us on

ancestor's cave

full of themselves

painting hunts and

handprints

spraying a message over a

stone age

how proud their bones must be to?

leave an

imprint for us in

this future to find

view   5

(zoom)   noir/blanc

not long from now

I will have this

view in focus and

clear in front of me

playing on the grassy field

there are always some ball and a

goal in mind

when I set out to

match the world

outside this focus

scratches   6

(focus)   noir/blanc

my back is

full of scratches as

chlorine burns the

focus to

my swim stroke like

crawfish pinching or

roaches clipping the

gang down the walk through the

watching birds from an

Audubon march leaflet stapled to the

inflatable telephone pole

floatation device

lean   7

(tripod)   noir/blanc

standing on the edge

looking across the breaking

ocean spray and froth

stings the eyes and melts the

shoreline shifts and

rips the glide of an

awakening

rider still sleeping above

staggering reefs and

seeing the weeds

lash and stay in place on the

lean of two legs

swimming through a

duck dive

bright   8

(darkroom)   noir/blanc

there is one bright

spot after another in the

night sky

turning over the course of the

night's shoot and

laughing at the escape

planning instead inside

this darkroom's

blank ceiling tiles

warping like a

folding blanket on the

bottom of an

aquarium's

bubbling chest open

chafe   9

(strap)   noir/blanc

last night's bar tab

should shake away the

fear of trails and

trials of circumstances

poising as beasts to

see a second chance the

burden is not in the

hands but in the

neck

surrounded by an imitation

leather stretching

chafing, chaffing to

hold the

shot in frame

petite   10

(flash)   noir/blanc

sleep petite

sleep, sleep

slumber, slump

I am awake from the

sound of your hum

heartbeat

skip, squish

your blood pulse

is alive from the

push of your heart

tiny drips

drip, drip

we are still breathing

bleeding from the swells of our tongues

please   11

(negative)   noir/blanc

I am pleased to

announce

that I will no longer

conceive the possibility of

happiness pursuing the

weddings of us as

time and place

abandoning my fears for

traveling back to the

age of

reasons to

let this be a

ring to

negotiate

foggy   12
(image)   noir/blanc

there was no peace before?
our births to this world
I was born the same
month and year as the
Vietnam War
ended for us
since then
we have been in a fog of wars in
all over the Middle East, Europe and
South and Central America
imagine a world without
resources

blurr   13

(lens)   noir/blanc

scurry into focus

little blurr

cannot see every

bit of you

flurried in your pixel's dust

float, fleet

flying above

below, sideways

out of sight in

frame to

  now

blind   14

(lights)   noir/blanc

I could not see through to the

next

weekend sleeping in

is the measure of

my stillness

resting is blind luck

doesn't shed a light on

how much oceans?

move every inch of

my eyes that

I saw you with

dream   15

(red light)   noir/blanc

why is that red light on?

awakening me to

you

so sweaty and sweet and

free of the dreams

connecting us to a

community of

saints and sinners

fighting and loving for

more time around

this puddled rock

rising and

falling from the ocean

collecting water in a

cycle of drops

dripping back to the ocean

spring   16

(pixels)   noir/blanc

we will not follow the

spring at all

its invention of summer

this the fall of

all things

bright and blight full

it pinches a little to

feel this

formula develops into a

side effect of

labor and lust in a

pixel's lore of

winter

logical   17

(digital)   noir/blanc

logic steady stare

binds the webbing

against the grain of the

algorithms across the

pulses of

1's and 0's

yes and no the

glass fiber optics

wider than the sky

larger than the planets

ranging further than

Pluto's dimming stature

mental   18

(clicks)   noir/blanc

we have this extra

time to click through

our cache and

watch our moments

freeze for us still

I am ready to let

our memories live

inside my molecules for a

few seconds the

mental holds the

silicate alive before

we rush back for more

wait   19

(still)   noir/blanc

do you also feel?

weight stills the inside

world

framing the air by a

wire and a

nail

do you also think?

that this wine will flow

pouring out more time

than air on a

glass and a

stem

space   20

(stream)   noir/blanc

more than enough

space to

be within and

any other time?

I snap back into this stream

evaporating

vaping

floating into another

place saturating the

space between the

sky and the

earth

spinning faster than its core

tap   21

(card)   memory

you see?

it is all you have

left to top off the

yesterday's

daydreams next to the

thoughts of

longing and yes

writing on a card to

bring back to the

familiar the

family of

images compacting

dark   22

(cloud)   memory

notwithstanding the

collection of moments

left in the air to

meander down from the

darkness to

light up the day

you remember when and for

how long?

clouds could hold on to

water and turn to re-

turns

scan   23

(stick)   memory

you scan the

scenery

your background

your backyard

believing the truth

will set the plea and

beg to not

be that bent

stick holding the

past in a

fraction of a

refraction of a

rock in the

stream of online

Apple Mysteries (1-3)

something was eaten

something was drunk

something was said

something was seen

To a primordial world comes the

burden of an Epoch where

myths turn monsters into

apples and apples become the

sacred stories found buried

online in that great abyss; the

red, yellow, blue, green, purple and orange

spheres gazing back at you

freeing the geist into an

art form.

1. Manifest series
(Atlantica as)

(forethought)

stealing the red from

fire off the green of the

mountain sides to re-

create mankind in an

offbeat chance of

bolting of lightning

capturing the

cataclysm of a stories passing

exploiting the eternal external

pseudocarp for the trick of

claiming the inedible haw and

fruit of a sacrifice instead of

beating the masses for the

theft of the reddening fire so

sown into that green mountainside

(is an arc of)

blues and whites of lightning

descending the

ages inside a yellow beam as

husbands and wives to

sons and daughters

building an allure to

survive in an apple

that throws seeds into the

green lands

changing their

advocation to harshness in

forms and with the

masses growing into

human beings the

beginning is an

emergence of more

mothers and fathers

(boxes)

metering quince without
 ever giving the women a
name after the
gift of stolen red flares begins to
pseudocarp for the
booming expanse of the
molding green
lush-ish blue of the
earth as the first to
fruit into
silver berries
embroidering veils of blooms
ornate in crowns of leaves
alluring other women to
un-naming the wonder that
was presuming sheer guile

(floral)

ranging the genesis of

mountains greening and

sacrificing in the

occurrences of

seeding the drupe's

preservation as the

remains of a

name giving up the

yellows and oranges of the

seeds in burnt

offerings to the

house and

hearth resounding a

translation of the whole

offering to the passage of the

levelheaded view that

appears between the

consequences

(drupelets)

ranging from the

maps of the borders between

regional reddish apples and

deep blue seas in a

biodiversity that is a

rose risen

arising to

prominence

notifying its rich

flora that the

admiration of its

greenish frames whitening the

clouds with

rain and wind

topping off the

planting across the

valley streaming into the

myths of distance

(girdling)

giving birth to the

authority over the

haw enticing the

verge of enough to

be several types of the

nine labors worthy of

retrieving the

stripes from the waist and

cuts away the

abducting

fermenting foments

falling in love with the

ceremony of rot too

drunk and still drinking

separating the accounts that

lead to the incidents of

slaying to the point of

wishing favorable light to

engage and contain a

fresher fruit juicy

(orange)

making one's appearance
endow a certain
mysterious power of
assuming every form of
balance

incarnations
are numerous and
commonly found in the
conceptions that
similarly
conceive numerous
rejections and
endorses forms for
prudent hearts

deep down crossing
over into the embodiment of
being another form
eternity is into the tempered
unconditional

un-conditioning

conditioning

infinitude of

finite sowing

layering down the

burden of

peopling and

revering

their grains and

achievements of

landing in the epithet

(brighter purple lighter)

falling in love again with a
story twice staged by
one amnesty
sowing a steadfast and
devotional hipster into life

rejecting one
version of falling in love and
accursing the
results of fright and
dragging in the belief of curses
guilty of killing soils from
its source of
revenge

(grape harvest)

these ritual yields ecstasy

fertilizing the culture of

worshipping at an early age

tracing forms describing the

arrival of a cult like

classical original

growing along the

great green mountain

sides with

youth and mortality

dying and rising up

naked and triumphantly discovering the

wild unfolding

branches dancing and

escaping the seasons for the

un-forcible exposure

(rooting)

meaning green

green earth

cleansing itself of the

produce that flows

out of the rivers into the

worship and swimming with the

pregnant pause so

secret

it wills the re-

birth of chaos and

fermentation that this

red fruit dangles in

offering up a self-

consciousness

fears of caresses for

consumption of flora as

proof of growing up

(alternately)

sacrificing fruit

is a giant spell casting

breath for

life cycles

no more kernels to invade

just laws inscribing

yellow fields that

show through their greening

treating gifts as grey rocks to

vanquish the figures with

red and blue detailing

time clasping its fist

mad like rust in the

veins coming out of the

other side to the

immortality of method

(green with the)

head of a nut
body of a man
delving into the center of a
design constructing a
genetically altering flight of
fancy fantasy

competing to rule the
beauty of sacrifice in a
show of depth in the
offspring with no
natural nourishment to
devour its substances

advice is for the gigantic
succinct curse of
machinery copulating in an
obscure travail and
burdening the
reproach to the assuming to
be several fruitful

seasons longer

(artful)

skill is the supply

transferring the stories about

rum running alone without

mentioning a wide

dazzling plane of

inventing production

already realizing

envisioning a

singular plane

beginning and

ending

finely crafting an

opening into each peach

consider this the

long term

consequences of creating an

almost impeachable portrait of

growth and gain

(wax and)

feathers with the

wings come together

warning of complacency

versus flight into the

melting seas

lapping into a

half-

prison

half-

born

half-

apple in your eye

stringing an

attachment to the full bunch

too close

too much further along

flopping under

nearly a bare spell en

route to a

lover's fair

(afterthought)

is another seed breaking the
prestidigitation of
human kindly
greening the atlas
not shrugging but
casting the
traits among the
responsibility for the
time to en-
vision and guide a
civilized pear into a
red fire glare

2. Found series
(Americano as)

(1)

hex and bane are a

must for the identity

crisis of the social

forefront of the exploited

twice born

reforming the gathering in a

lull that is

swelling into an

excavation of the

unifying field

theory of love and

life in a false

fruitful recess

blinding

(2)

whiskey is in the

glory of the

identifiers as

just in themselves

adapting into the

unchanging and always

adding details of

linking the strength with

courage of the unmasking

ingenuity as the

prowess of the labors with

trickery just like

blue skies that are

preventing a playful

respite

(3)

slayers are the days that

behead and spare parts a-

long side of

pools with quince in a

wasteful alluring

slack hand that

restores the available

charms of a

descend

exposing

occupation of the bearers

drunk on the burnt

ashes of these skillful

leisures

(4)

prescribing an

attraction to the

sacking of a

thrill in hiding a

form of the enticing

shoring up of grace

engraving the time

imposing

attesting

lapping up the bourbon

well before the

origins that begin to

name the beguiling

ivy of the to

be spreading a small swell

stipulating the elusive

remaining day's reprieve

3. Create series
(Continuum)

(introducing an apple acting as)

secret order to

be informed of a split

engagement in the

founding of an entire act

glistening to carry it out with

calumny that are

both religious and royal as

astute systemic

elimination of a

history and thought that

preserves the self-

evident lack of

detractors paving the

way for the high

value sources of

political challengers for

hire as

professional killers

(1) posthumous)

gleans the

surge as it

lures in the rushing of the

bay as a gift to the

skeptical sky and

sacrifices the

lost to claim being a-

live affords a

morning of mourning

searching for loathing in a

harmless thigh and a

zany beast with that

toothy grin from a

libel mouth like

shrapnel pills scraping the

pelt with a tongue

yesterday and

carrying it in to the

future on its

shoulders to the infancy of infamy

(2) revenge)

sounds out the clay that

covers your

mouth from poisonous fumes

fame says to terrorize the

germane of notoriety

cutting off the harvester of

struggles that arc

not the elite but the idea of

winning within hints of the blue sea

sky is vaulting the

poison onto the red

skin of a firebrand's form

(3) surviving the red of)

affluent's anger is as

red as the stigma of a

glinting doom and gloom

not to say it but to

overcome or out-

run the sleeping hind and seek

not the cumbering or

encumbering with

desertification of a sacred

orchard containing claims of

being told and knowing the

apple's apparent

cynic and savior looking into

forgiveness as penance for the

spirit as minstrel's fool

(4) disappointment)

overcomes the

humiliation of

enabling the dangers of a

kind and hospitable

devourer of a raw

glittering attraction like

wine in a jar closely

drunk and attacking the

seep of a villainous retreat

top of a lulling is an

immortal volunteer whose

pain and torture

contradicts the freeing of a

visitation to catch the

respite that begs to

drive it bound and down

(5) stable and)

clean too
intently for impressions of
that humiliation and
malice in the
quirkiest and
juiciest apples

life in a wash as
filth and care for
refusing the grounds to
reward the
case the re-
routes the claims of
paying for the
rush of alienating in
slanders akin to the
ruling of stillness as a
performance of awkward
eyes awaking

(6) toxic)

brooks of a
defamation sharply the
colorful currents of
migrating beams
flickering
quickly launching the
sacred relevance of the
ramble and scoot
ramble and shoot

yellow light still
flickers far-
off into the
field through the
countryside
filling up with the
crops and apples of the
deeming gleaming
meandering scene

(7) capturing)

censorship of a

permissive offering to over-

take the time a-

way from the

havoc of the rapidly

jet streaming to

sacrifice the

throttling it takes to

reflect upon the

pertinence of

wreaking valuable

assistance a-

way from the

sacrifice to a

candid rancor

(8) bluish flesh)

springs up to travel
back to help bring forth and
chase away the tethers of
awareness in a wild expelling breath

eaters of the eaten as a form of
revenge takes the flavors and
surges then into antipathy that
cuts the binding of reddening flesh to the
lore as the deep seas entrenching life

waters so blue fill the
mouths with shoots adeptly into ill-
willed dedications for
those who refuse a
glimmering decadence to this
sacrificial sham

(9) pleasing)

wanting to
retrieve the appropriate
inlet that full-
throated the offerings of
acrimony to
take down the agreements of
doubters with greenish apples that
explode in the microwaves of the
exploiting claims

thoughts turn plots into
wells alongside the returns of the
disguises in which a court
jester defines the
distrust of humiliation

(10)   obtaining the)

pessimists fulfilling the

identity and frustrations

given off by a sore red bite

heating its way into

conveyance of literal

sweating into action

landing a blow to the

undercut of the

denigration dealing with the

slayers of the spoils for

shapes and sizes

piercing the pods of the

hoards diving off the

alteration of an obsolete

repetition for the

swallower's sacrifice is

biting and scattering the

crossing out of these

words

(11)   completely)

claims that the

cleansing is the cost

paying for the

blue in the cove

doing more ill-

repute to steal the

sky in times and

locations of the

holiday's enmity

this task is

crushing it into the

startup of the

dissenters relating to the

contumely of an

alternating personality

who is fulfilling

instead of

emptying the

demonstrable void

(12)   guarded)

venom's fall

imitates the

entrance of a

guidance to come

unknowingly unsure those

who ably desire it

doom and ensure an

ignominy

preparing to stay in for the time being

tradition's insults of the

permission and

sacrifices the health to re-

release and liberate the

hospitality and

festivities of the

pseudo-carp of now

(concluding the apples are yellowish)

calling out to

commencement as a reflection for

minds to flow into

marshes into ponds into

becks and creeks 'til

rivers turn deltas into the

bight of a gulf

highly swampy is the

verge of the

sites to lambert in the

murdering and re-

sacking of a message

traveling the green-

green landscape

profoundly impacting the

spawning romance within its

literature and publishing its

connection to those as

obituaries of this time and place

Waves

to

Curl

Thankful I've spent my

life making this happy little

artwork otherwise I wouldn't

be able to live in this over-

looking the ocean of ideas

breaking under my eyes

through

my fingertips.

Waves

1.

golden in your eyes the

sun is in the

sky winking

I could never tell

you where you've been 'til now

only to show you about that

time you broke

your fall on the

front seat passenger side

bare beast with a

flare for yellow lines

blending the air waves of a

last glance

first chance to another

growth within the

timetable to play a

game time re-

mission with really

real deal feels

2.

born from the vix

vapid $6

trillion away from today

we'll invest in

our debt like an

unloaded bump stock

aimed at a

fairground for

rednecks and sunsets

raining truckloads of

bitcoins operating

algorithms splashing that

cash in a wrapped up

refill bill primed to

Skynet the last

hasta la vista

jobbing the binary of

Alexandria and

Edison's electric

generalizations of

labor saving devices

3.

this is no tragedy

yet

this is the sin of

not being worried about a

soapbox

slathering up

near minty conditioning to

stand up online

along a

wavy lazy

days of summer

time blue skies that

are trolling across the

miles of a blessing and

feeble attempt at a

date night

4.

late

tonight

is only a cheesy

stringy tight rope

theory from

your pizza toppings

listed in chronological

ordering online

delivery taxing

driverless horseman of a

osmosis smartphone

picking up aisles of

sleeping 'til noon-

ish on a

Saturday

here in the parking lot

causing a pasta

fixation that

waves to carry

words into the minds of a

promo flickering

no longer driven by the

desire to

leave a kiss through the

windshield

5.

we sit back and

enjoy a blank screen

shadow puppets of

popcorn poppers that

dampen lights fading into

screenplay producers of

mood and moon

signs for this to

come up again like the

moon and

tides and

reflections on a self-

sustaining life

devoid of its

reasons to linger

longer after glowing

our neon teeth

whitening

together along with the

tale end of the real

measure of humidity of these

excessive exhales

6.

don't worry

I'll watch

another 10yrs. of

lucky at my age with these

knees and that hipster

I'll bend and not break

I'll do a long sigh and

strengthen our gains in

milk and honey

train these wax feathers to

strain through your hands and

face the lit-up neon of

twilight and brake lights

shimmering in the

breeze of another

bar bill spilling so

long to pour out a

plot twist

7.

it is the west at

last on scene

we change our eyes to

glance into the

geist and take a

stance on trivia and

knockdown the seats for

now is the time to

chime the mime to

hear them dream their

arte de comedy that's a

heart as a lonely healer while

orange clouds burn

red to purple sky

spotting the first

stars across the

windshield

8.

you lay there

pantomiming the moon rise

shaping the horizon to a

crescent heart coloring the

clouds that soak up the

blues of a fresher moon this

electromagnetic

field research

turn south to west

jump starting a

pace of yellow

dashes flushing the

magnetism of a

polar eclipse of the

sky high green waves in

your eyes

9.

our heads just above the dashboard

green waves break over

sets and

sets of molecules

sprinkling in

stars and the

moon and the

stars and the

stars

sifting waves through

our eyes lashing to the

sky to the

sky

we spin the

waves and

waves to the

stars

10.

I really

actually

don't even care

where the stars

are right now

tonight lives

dangerously under the

milk and waves that

mellow and stall

together along with the

distilling aerial

vibrations of an extra-

stellar lighting

sharing the laughs that

orbit around

each and all of

us

to

1.

no mass

setting the sun to

always rise to

fall against the curling

atmosphere of a new

age brand of

waves too cunning for the

lengths of selling

plot holies through

vapors and mists turn

mountain tops

bumping the

core of a being

line set to

music and dreams of

wishing wells

falling off this

cliff hanger

2.

below this

rust stops the curling of

time and space

that explains the feeling of

wellness fed up and

dead tired of the

choir telling tales of

dread and smelling

like an old wet cat waiting

waiting for waves to

stack linen and

slag condensing the

spirit on sparkling

charcoal and

clay about another

dimension to shine so

brightly into the

brilliance of still

stalling mercury from

drowning

3.

still

I reject nothing the

stillness

informs in magic of

this or that

I will be another in a

wave of

stars and

curls and

waves to

see

beyond the

tip of an open

hand swinging a

tin cup to the

sound of spam and

eggs and a side of

moon shine

Curl

1.

I am your new best

imagining friend

wander*wonder*why

I will eclipse

your moon too

see

your stars and

spin and spin and

breathe beneath

your namaste

have a nice day and

play the wind

driving rain into

my skin so deep as

secrets of the

past grasping for

your eyes sideways

laughing up the

weeds in a new

kind of fame

one that will help

stare into the night sky and

sleep

2.

it doesn't take all

 night to uncurl the

waves in your eyes

this book

these little songs

fortified by the strength of

winds forcing the

sun beams to hold onto the

gravity just for a

minute

generously

hums in-

between gusts and

myths of light over

head and

laughing and

eating pie

we stake our

gravity to these wind

3.

speech so easy

I am not like a

coiled up

Telsa

electrified in

arches between the

wake of an

introvert slipping

still

still

reaching above as

below the

real reals

displaying the days

I long to be

asleep in the

burnt off

booster of a

pleasure prophecy

4.

I curl up around your

eyes

sighs

laughs

dancing

birthing a dream of

trying to

place that pulse and

space under the

milky sway tonight

winding from the

stray in me

playing us in a

sit calm rom

Freudian daydream nation

5.

silk curls the

velvet of desire

full of tears and

golden stars

shining the

shimmer in

hops for hips or

spasms

breaking the

heft in my heart

wildly embedding the

orbit in

verse and clock-

work that

unties the lining with

platinum ties

lying down the

tracks of a too

often posting of concrete

cracking platitudes

6.

you're twisting the curl

down your long neck-

lace tracing the

freckles into a

spectacle of star-

light

deep in the plot

singing along to the

dreams another dream of

streaming consciousness

3 days ago these

icicles

shared the

fluids

dripping down the

landscape of your

back in a flash

flood of dash lights

dancing

7.

there is probably no

more that I could say but

today's another play at this

stage of our lives

where I'm just

hanging lights on the

curls from my

pen on this word pulp

knowing where to begin a

confetti confessional

never too natural

nurturing kindly the

model citizen

reacting to a

poor constitution on a

rainy day into a

cool night

declaring my heart-

beats faster than

your breathe

8.

you stretch the

curl off the

bend in the road

remembering the wild-

flower spied while

listening to the

time before

analog bumps and

bangs digital

stars popping the

fizz of the

drizzle off the

windshield

9.

your legs

swing, swinging

swing from the

laptop spring

springing into a

fall full of

coins billing

tolling you over the

moon and back

its good to see

you curling on a

cushion from the

glare of a

text tracking the

distance in-

between a server and a

meme stocking

up on a wish-

list and

rock candy kisses

10.

I too

am a stranger

now that the world's

found another

Atlantis

I am the bearer of

casseroles and

beans in which to

dip with a factory

coat staging the

end of times in the

bubbles of champagne

well wishes and

cavalier dreams

dancing a bat shit

crazy grinding out the

last chance to take

hats off as part of our

online identity crisis

curling up to the

wealth of nations

like dande-

lions from the concrete

Hamilton Street collection

a graphene projection of
a poet's life written in
a libertine's voice

Part 1
a graphene projection of
a kite's flight reeled in
a libertine's life
sand and (fabled)
ports

1 - you

were two years younger
than me

my hover
my friend

we will raise
parallel boards to
hold in the sand

2 - I did not build this

they dumped the sand on
our driveway late one morning in
spring

you were not there when we
climbed to the top of the sand
pile and hung on the net of
our basketball hoop

it took my family that
saturday to load
unload and reload the
red wheelbarrow between the frame
nailed together the weekend before

3 - my own

you
holding a yellow shovel
digging
      pouring
digging
      pouring
smiling at me while I set
rows of green army men
opposite rows of gray army men

your hair was not quite blonde
not quite brown

I wonder if there was a difference
sky was bright and blue and the
air is warm with the
smell of fresh leaves and sand

one fist full of sand
made a mound of
our spent time in this box
that builds us as each speck of
sand is another cell dividing

4 - you find this moment

picking up the
sand between your fingers

you were
still for a moment
smiling with your eyes on the
sand on the side of a hole
that rolls some of the
sand back to the
bottom

you scooped it up again and
carried it to the top of the
growing mound outside the box of
sand

thousands of tiny bits of
quartz and sediment tumbled and
swelled and twinkled the mound's
steepening incline

I looked at the shine in
your eyes as I laid my right
ear onto another pile of
sand

world looked not like
it has but
what it will be,
angles of differences leaned me back on
my back

sky saw me between the
tree branches
up there

I had yet to climb

I saw a string of clouds behind a
plane and wondered
what it would be like to

be a kite above us all

Part 2

a graphene projection of

breath's flight distilled in

a libertine's life

boom city busts

we walk in from the roar of

thunder through the gallery of

harsh lighting before the

storm's end drenches the

soles of our soaked

down strides

some girls sway in from the

front with a strong mind to

stop time and play along the

side of the red stained bar as

we slide onto the matte black

vinyl stools

beer and whiskey chase down the

end of the last one

we are the

slender look of hello the

slow taps pour out the

new chances in a tender

service of drunken streams

that sway and settle on the

hardwood bar

currents in the beer foam form the

length of a drink and

stabilize our handshakes that

shiver bold knows to everyone

I tell all of space and time that

plays between the drench and rest

she drinks down a flirt and

pops up onto the bar

she plays the buttons of her shirt open

one by one

everyone in the bar is

watching as her bra slips from

her shoulders into the air

nothing as beautiful as this until her friends

grab and pull her flesh sparkling off the bar

her friends collect her

clothes as the rest of the crowd

throw boos through the cheers

memory's screen over the course of the

day now distant in me more

than the depth of the floor

2 - here

neon signs radiate off the

varnish onto the slick skin with

its salt that refracts the

whole atmosphere to a

stand-still born shots

we swim into the sink below the

shift in the room's belief in the

circumference of time between

drinks and pours

just as the wake settles in the

next round the spray of

words rise from our stools

I hold myself up above the

dim lights to dissipate the

night 'til now

another sip vanishes between the lips

we sit sopping up the

parts of us that are

already tomorrow through the

sweet stagnate disposal of

rest and the

stormy night

we risk here to split like

water into Oxygen's breath the

sips and spills into the

sleepless drifts the

city licks and lips

it is that simple the

midnight blue night

light moon floats on the

looks and distance between the

two old boys at the end of the red bar

I giggle at their young

thoughts on old ideas while I remain

neutral within this calm brewing into the

pours over sores

then one boot kicks and the

other's head snaps

back against the bar rail

everything stops except the

boot and the head that keeps

bashing and crashing 'til an arm

pulls the body of the boot away

we witness the young head

throbbing thin black and neon blood that

pools red on the black matte vinyl stool

this is not a reason why

this is the slow step on the stall of a

mellow real tune that plays on the

satellite truths casually above the

stool still staining the floor with

his blood dripping blood

3 - we Are

my arm raises my can over
my neck bending a sip from a
smile that brings a newfound
fondness for emptiness inside
I ready my breath for those words

we speak to us in a new day and
our stools sputter and slide and groan
this time belongs to our leaving within the
wraps of coats and cover words
we wish there was more in enough time to
do this all the same again

we start back down the lighted gallery
passing through the ceiling fan and
mirrors in these currents and reflections
we look straight past us and
extinguish each step's rhythm

now is broken down into

syllables that laugh and sing through the

stories of our short rise and quick falls

no moon could wash the dawn away

our puddles with tree branches

this hour's old yesterday tells us

we are no longer the day before us with a

stable notion of our tides and time

I feel my head

my blood flow back and forth

we know our place

when the light cracks open the

6 a.m. start to the flesh tones of the

sun rise to quell the swell in our

eyes and carry us over the wash of

quick kisses

handshakes and

traffic lights glow to the flow from

our own gravitational pull

Part 3

a graphene projection of

a finch's flight instilled in

a libertine's life

playlist for the
flight home

(I see you)

"And she was"

"Always on my mind"

"Tangled up in Blues"

(Ok)

"I'm going home"

"the Walk"

"can't find my way home"

"Say Goodbye"

(I pass)

"Carnival of sorts (Boxcars)"

"Castles made of sand"

"Just like heaven"

(and)

"Thirty-Three"

(wave to)

"Freedom of '76"

"Pablo Picasso"

"Bukowski"

(the ground 35,000 feet below)

Part 4

a graphene projection of

an arrow's flight filled in

a libertine's life

[eros 6 a.m.)

introduce

slabs of
concrete meet under
my feet

I am told to be
grateful for
each one I walk to

I am the
root of
this earth in
moving
deserving to
be here with the present
smiling at me as the
sun

1-[1

--pressure--

pop his ears

decompress from the
solid land beneath him

graceful thoughts
slide into the
disembarking courage to
face a new road to
see her again

--awaken--

winding through the
terminal in a
crowd
eager to sort
their luggage

he picks up his
leaving for her and
leave

--concrete--

meeting
leading under the wheels
metering his pulse

he is
no longer
brave but
willing

--kisses--

today
marks the day
he loathes only the
length between
their arms
touching a
complicated assembly of
simplicity

their eyes are
tenderness
moving the distance between
their breath and
snickers

--the sweat--

rises through the skin

she ignores the
dreams of
death
that stumbles in
her eyes and

she listens to her
young heart beat

--shadows--

hold the
light dancing along the walls
red
yellow

green into
blue
spinning over them
passing them a-
long for the
the light

just dancing and
playing with her
delicate heart

--accustom to--

he strives for
stars and a pluto to
guide the night by
glancing at the warmth of the
danger of not leaving

--his back—

cracks on crisp sheets
holding him open in
front of her

she tilts her head and
smirks at his heart's
rapid and coarse
repeat

--she lays--

down under
windowpane's clear light

she laughs
not that

she can but
just can

--a touch--

her cheek
softly exposes the
curve of
her delicate
glance into the
humidity of
his and her words
that belong in between
their goodbyes and leaving

2 - compose

--sparks--

glaze looks
she knows the
climate
exciting inside
brings her an
absence of sense

--brilliant--

composures of
unease leaning towards
sleepiness
he finds himself
lost again

their laughter

cradling each other's
not knowing

--talk of--

living now lies in
eternal lighting from
sparks no more in
his stars for
today

--now--

hangs over her like
a newborn tear
repelling down
her face
leaping off her jaw
free

--breathe in--

morning dust in the
sunlight
now living for
her smile
laughing again at
yesterday

casual a
distance the
sun wakes up

--the air between--

them shines
more and more

they admire
each bit of other

today the
same way as
many they hope
they will memorize

--the light--

is her smile and
laughter at the
courage
it takes to be

smiling back
they try to serve
each other's happiness
belonging to now
more than before

--drives--

pavement too
soft and wet before
approaching
their car

songs start and
surround them as
they flirt
their touch to taste

--care into--

mornings
stretching into

weekends of
even softer and
sweetness
caresses

they love each and
every part of
their being together

--dreams--

fall asleep
holding their
comfort still

they wake up
beloved

--home--

begins again
while
driving away

still thinking about the
all of her

3- to

--time--

likes to sleep through
some afternoons 'til to-
night is the moon
awakening to the

sound of the
phone's tone
confessing the
blandness and
bore of being
apart

--speeds--

slows the
arrival of her
waiting to
push the delivery
driving under the
overpasses and
streetlamps

faster isn't enough

--still--

he wonders if
last night wasn't enough to

desire is more than
just today

it is one more chance to
be more for years

--shines in --

her hair
flares down
his will to
struggle over dinner

he wishes
he could help her
right now
but first
he must clean
his spill
his soul

--urges--

are louder than
his red and green reasons for
faith and
ever after

gold ring
brings them back to
their new
newer life

--ease to--

soothe his
reluctance to
preserve presence
giving him the
place to
displace

his cell phones
weighs less
than his answers
today

--lengthen--

shorten to a

new found
fondness for
laughter

--the look--

will and the
want in the
light of the
growing
glowing
warmth of
their survival
together

4 -- congeal)

--spring in--

scents around them
belongs to them
more than less as
they are reaching for
their breath

--tonight--

she talk about
her resemblance to
another time
passed

--last night--

he talked a

version of the
distance to travels through the
future

--boils to--

blind to the
brilliance of
their luster the
un-polished as
their heart craves

--pieces--

are tearing
flowing down
her face
making today the
most dangerous
day of his life
that leaves her a
puddle of
electricity

5 - us

outside

6 am
angels in the
kitchen light tell her
he is still
her red shifting stars
scratching the
back of this

night's sigh

stars scrap across

speckled
darkness before the
spectrum of the
sunrise
heals at the
speed of sight

overhead

he lifts her
laughter into the
yellow light between
their haze and the
play combined in
their parts

their fingers trace

lock of
if they will not
holding back the
barriers
that keep
them together

conclude

we
are pebbles of light

some soft
some bright

wishing that we
will beyond
our lives

we
are electricity

some hum
some whelp

pulsing us through
time beyond
our years

Part 5

a graphene projection of

a kite's flight reeled in

a libertine's life

sand and (fabled) ports

5 (A) dust in the air (Metal, Rocks, Plastics, Blood, Bone)

I was a worker

your lover a

painter a

force multiplier

Indigo

you

Carmine

we're not here in

this dusty

blown up

dried up

alluvium

constricted by

mountains and sky

I'm still older than you

I radio in the daisy cutters in on

jet engines spinning white

lines behind them

my laser focus beams
lightning flashes before
thunder explodes metal and
bone and heart and souls

so many
so few
rise within the dirt
dust and sand
smoke
plastic and rocks

I can no longer hear the cries
just feel the wheezing
gasping sighs

5 (B) my chest full of sand (expand and contract)

I lay back and

breath it in and out

(bone, blood, plastics, rocks, metal)

dust

bleeding in and out of the

side of my chest

my lungs

coughing

coughing

drowning in

sand

6 — uncovery

it has taken me a long

time since my recovery and

you are still no longer with us

I am back in country in

my state across town a

crossroads in my cousin's Super Bowl

party eating chili

hummus and salsa

we talk about the

T.V. the

false starts and smooth finishes

after the game

when most of the party leaves the

few of us left in the garage

vape and giggle about silly shit

my smile just grows and

grows and I tip over sore from

vaping and giggling at silly shit

7 - salt mine

this is our sweat in our tears

that gathers under the growing

ruins that circulate through us

we live on/with this salt on

our skin within

our bodies

lit by

our minds

that shine straight through the

blood

that is our work

Part 6

a graphene projection of

sweat's flight spilled in

a worker's life

salt

waking up

this is no doomsday

        village

this is where artisans and

engineers and

singers labor

where tasks

        plant with a

strong handle on

            our production from

blood and salt in

our skin the

            routes of

convenience

this land beneath us the

forms of extremes

        yields the

crop of us as

raw as our sources on

our backs

we carry the buy and

sell culture

do we quiver before the

               market or

     hold it all in

peace?

    we build

       this idea

           deep in the soil

hoping for rain inside the

          sunlight

across town

nine hours after
I assemble parts the
sweat builds over
my groggy thoughts

my car gags a
start and the
engine mutters
Prometheus

I shuffle through radio
stations as I feel for
my seat belt strap

first gear is on the left and
my right hand finds it
without too much fuss

rolling forward
I plunge the clutch to
pause the car

reverse

always reverse

grinds in my ears and in the

gears

new gear gives a roll

back an angled attempt to

escape this parallel

finally

forward

I move down the street

turn a

turn a

road goes down the

ramp into the

expressway

lot

I pull into the lot

almost blocked by a

semi backing into the

loading dock

I slid my car on gravel to a

spot facing the

street through a chain linked fence

engines settle for the day and

rests after I turn my

car off and step my body out

I kick loose gray stones a-

long the gravel at the

loading dock and

punch in the clock

then slid my time card

back into its slot

my boss spots me and points a

finger to signal the

need for me to lift and

pull a trunk load of

metals and vinyl and glass

already unloading

fine without me

when the hours pass

gray floors paint

chips under my boots as

I shuffle back and

forth on the line

seven screws and a

driver lays

next to an almost

assembled door

I pull my gray

leather glove up

my hands to feel the

screen wires bend

salt drips in my eyes

one of the ten

or so

I will

handle until lunch

unloads a lunch break

our trunk bought

sandwiches unwrap around

lips at the break table

conversations that reveal the

repetitions of this

lunchroom assembly that slaps and

smacks like the saws and

drills drone on

then the sudden sound of

"Fuck You!"

unsettles our food down on the

tabletop shock

we get up and shift our way to the

loading dock to look

there In the

middle of Mt. Elliot a

young man is swaggering away

he raises his arms up above a

black metal 9 above a

faded white tank top and

turns to us

"What the Fuck are You looking At?"

my simulacrum stills

we unload our eyes from

his stare and break quickly

back into the pale gray light in the

cinder block room

Orange's Codices

(blueprints 1-5)

To construct a world with the
burdens of Epoch where
legends turn structures into
house and homes become the
sacred sites found buried
online in that great abyss; the
orange, purple, green,
blue, yellow and
spheres gazing back at you
freeing the forms into
art.

1. One who comes in Peace
   (igneous)

   "the web-priests may give
   offering to you, LOL, the
   web-priests may stretch to
   you their arms with
   libations on the site, as it
   was done for HipHop with the
   remains of the imbibing cups."

volute bristles to the internet and
architect of the step-pyramid a
web-priest in the figure of the sun
glorifying and deifying death

   polymath of a décor
   who was a
   poet a
   judge an
   engineer a
   magician a

scribe a

physician an

astronomer an

astrologer and an

owner of a tomb with

engraved libations

written as ritual among

statues and status

collecting intellectuals in a

death cult

distinct epithet

inspirit

inscriptions unfinished salacious

abandoning the embellishment of rain

falling, acquainting with the upright

architecture and

mathematics of the other

patrons and scribes

merging within a

titillating culture

linking and revering a

stimulation of the mythic

mortals consorting with the

chains of machines at the

base endings between the

rise of the sun and the

lunula dreams of the

starving moon

2. Fire lit river of Mercury
   (metamorphic)

Mercury white sulfur
construction is a callow
situation underneath the
truth baiting of role
models dividing into a
face off the raw
core of a carved-out coffin

adornment is a fully
sealing source of the
tracers of light containing the
layers of a
bronze whetting
hundreds of upstanding
encrustations into
overlays priming a shot of
mercury lit up into the
candle's yellow flickers
burning red firing

quickly turning the

silver mechanics of a

river building craftsmen

who divulge treasures and

inappropriate constellations of that

extinguishing the construct of

traps for all naïve workers to

resemble in their ceremonies

dig through the layers of the

blundering ground waters

looting the rebellion of the

burning down concrete

underground streams as

solid evidence of a fire

green and blue to the

torch hand worthy of

suffering large-

scale scholarships

whose tracer's grasp of

frills in fragments of the

folderols and their

golden polished cockade

digging a well into the

greenish blue earth with the

bronzer overlaying the

red terracotta on a

gold brick carrying in

hydraulic carts with

silver cases in a

vantage point of

sale of a commercial re-

purchasing of the gifts and

talents designating the

excavation of

wood and pyre

erecting the pit of sulphate

drilling meters in mounds

3. Placed of the Retreat
   (sedimentary)

dating back to a
structure with the
volume of the world
surrounding it

raining)

seasons and
melting snows are a
confluence of the
results in the
perennial streams of
layers upon
layers of texts in
yellow bolts of
lost lightning

existing in the roles of
primary connection

centering on an

outpost locating and

linking those posts to

classical alum

consuming the

scrupulous alkali

noting a dying breed of

techniques as diverse in

colors as prevalent in

materials as they are

contemporaneous designs

seeming to avoid the

fate of water logging deposits

stylistically resembling the

murex of the period of

stains in a

still beating heart

inlaying a cranial scan in

exchange for the highest

plateau of pleasure

popularizing the velvet

acolyte of the skin

manicuring a saffron

claiming the gathering of

folderols and

nibbles on the

temple of thought

processes

layering)

volume in terms of the

structures size and

resembling the

superposition of the

temple's precepts to

point out the perpendicular in a

citrus and swerves

no longer reassembling the

style of stares on

all fours with purpura

swelling

expanding and

exposing every direction of a

full frontal lobe in a

full context grid as an

underlying deviation of thought

relating to the yellow solar

pommel still imparting today

stylistically common to

reflect on the surface tension

drinking carmine and the

inebriation of

jade cacti juicy

liquid wells up in the

molded re-

construction fire of

yellow to

red to

green to

blue

suggestions of a

unique brain fogging a

plane white pedal

roughly finishing the

horizon

vertical

digital

dialogue

tracing)

thinly

ideas of

blue to

green to

red to

yellow

elements of style

looping the gimmick to

sample the noise

carrying over through the world

4. Genio huius Loci

(gaseous)

genitive – the instance of

denoting a case of

nouns and pronouns

genius of the place, fascination

street, numia, legion

cohers, a la, closer to me

centuria, praetarium, castra

volcanoes, love cats, vexillae

jupiter, juno, genius principis

subdividing, just like heaven

sow, daemons, genii, guardian

angels, gens, djinn

genie, genius, lullaby

individual instance of

general divine nature

presage

                    cunina – of the cradle

potent

                    cube – lying down to
sleep

reap

                    rumuna – of breast
feeding

radii genii shrines in the

home just below the Mt.

agatho daemon (good demon)

inside a snake ball

ancient practice of leaping a

propitious house snake

companions which controls the

natal star, the gods of

human nature, in that she is

mortal for each person with a

charging expression

black and white

spitting from birth

genius of patrons of

freemen, owner of homes

patron of guilds, philanthropist

official, villages, other divinities

relatives, friends of the

genius and honor of the

instances of genitives denoting the

case of nouns and pronouns

taking an action verb in the

battle between evil and

evolutionary success

5. Unquenchable Curiosity

(plasma)

An)

inventor a

painter a

sculptor an

architect a

scientist a

musician a

mathematician an

engineer

etc... a

writer a

geologist an

anatomist a

botanist a

historian a

cartographer an

astronomer

helicopter yellow fin spin into a

parachute's red flare

drifting down into a

submersible aqua green under a

gliding blue sky clouds

primary colors are dispiriting-

ly remote only

empirical scales of

depth as an

unquenchable curiosity

feverishly inventing an

unorthodox artist as a

study of the

decent without

precedent and

most parodies of

portraits in the

renaissance primarily as a

cultural greening of idols honestly

surviving the nature of de-

composition in

notebooks containing the

red hot malleable of re-

purposing the

production of the mechanical

ingenuity is a

conceptualizing

centralizing

design of a

feasible fancy for

manufacturing a number of

role models and heads-

up displays

texting the strengths of

discovering nowadays

homestead is a

household of legitimately

honorably known

modern scene of

latin and

geometry in a

red blade dripping from the

sky blue in a

heart piercing form of a

monster spitting flames at the

legends of carbon

boiling down the

Orange's peel means

be)

      an apprentice in one of the

      finest studio plays that

      lead to the worshipping of an

      exposing vast range of

      skills like

            drafting

            casting

            drawing

            painting

            sculpting

            modelling

            a la carte

            working on

mostly a yellow angle

holding a green velvet robe in a

manner of a superior

brush stroke

qualifying now as a

master setting up in a blue

workshop drawing room with

pen and ink that

witness a hand

full of red modelling clay

seeing a)

      liar's silver recording that

      creates a feasible charge of the

      independent emissions of

      altarpieces competing in

      many diverse fields

      traveling marvelously through

      taxation expenditures and

      employing floats of

      red clay horseheads

      casting a huge aside to the

      surpassing inside the

planning of bronzer

canon to practice

targeting that wins the

methods of attending a

grass greening festival

these maps are

producing a town

plan rarely

conceiving today's

construction projects in a

strong-

hold standing

supplying water to

painting blue and green in a re-

location next to a

mural prominent for

including a figure of the

act of survival in and

around this way

death)

now both are active at this

time to be revealing a vapid

cluster of lives with a

pension for mechanical

strokes consisting in an

accordance with the

public remains of a

diagnosis purely in red

interring in a

partially-

complete skeleton's

yellow sun faded chest with

stone green fragments

attributing to a

tomb's reflection in a

sky blue

skull cap

locating an

excavation poet

Wolves

&

Lions

(24 little songs dreaming)

1.

what is the subject

what is the verb

do they

agree with the

object of your

flagrant

selfish

reliance on

water

do they make

us feel like

we are

liberating our

sense of every-

day re-

freshing of the

mundane to

sustain such an

appeal

2.

poolside

mojitos

deep divers and a

hysterical

channeling of

survivalism as a

lifetime subscription to

warmer weather

birds of a

feather prancing

together with

one night

chancers to the

depth

holding their

breathes

3.

cabana towels

smooth out the sweat

I left drinking and

thinking about the

game day delivery of

just like that

last winning

I saw the sun pay the

phone that played my

favorite songs as my

neck rises to

smile at the

light and

lap up a

glass or two of

mix drinks

4.

tender is the

buttons with which

pitchforks and

torches trigger on-

line tensions of

daylight savings and

holding back a

flood of toxins

no one wills the

waves to wave

these bro's and

foe's express a

need to

nurture their child-

hood desire without

consenting to the

tides

5.

wind is

just a breezy

breeze

show me the

geography of the

lush trees and

birds and

bees in the

anatomy of the

south sea of the

jet stream

washing the

twisting through a

over rushing

amount of

currency

6.

sinking steep in the

depths of another

pour down

finding out the styles of

wooden beams

deconstructing the sense of longing

it scratches out of the

sand arming a

squint of light

showing off the

world like a

high schooler lounging in

my only thought today

is to have or

have not a

lasting thirst so

sweet

7.

what does a diamond

look like under the

weight of the

world

it beats back the

pressure with a

stronger bond

worthy of a

gold ring

playing house with

hearts

beating faster and

faster than the

grass roofs

starting to

slicken from

rain

8.

there is something in the

air tonight

hold on to it

I think

I see it

feel it

flash bang it

phrasing a

portage never to

equal the distance to this

moment of time

I must live in this

moment

there's no

alarm

when I

need it

9.

how hot is too

much warning

how wet is

enough already

could we even

conceive of the

ocean or any

other notion

rapid firing

super soakers

raining supreme

full of grace and

spasms on the

beach front

economy into the

moon lit escape

plan of the dunes

10.

there's a

simmering

darkness

starting to

paddle across the

puddles

splashing under the

soles of my

feet soaking

wet

lapping up the

darkness of a

silver lining

silver bullet

banding together to

gather a storm

11.

stars rain out the

dreams and streams of

night and

youth

cleansing out the

stabilized whole while

others ride out

centuries in a

wardrobe full of

windbreakers over

silk suits

claiming I summoned the

wolves and

lions to a

debt collection

12.

why did I just dream

I was at Gary Snyder's

house in the suburbs of

my mind with

thankfulness and the

most beautiful bird of

paradise

I've ever seen

shitting on Gary's out

stretched hand as

he smiled and

laughed like it was a

peacock grouse

letting go of a

Picasso

Pollack

potluck

13.

here's a little

bittie about

Ann and the

death of Jack in an

alcohol soaked

tale of a coyote

tripping over a

road to nowhere and

everywhere fast in

blues and middle age

coming down

easy under

weak knee benders and

beats of their

own dreams

hurling madness at

their success at

100 mph

14.

   then rain

   came in like

   lions and the

   wolves in a

   litter biting

   hungry

   howling

          roaring

                 flashing

          booming

   soaking the

                 drenching

   ditching the

   starlit and moon full

   beaming like a

   turning classic

   black/white

   chaser

15.

still the wind

howls and

swats the branches

down the streets as

power flickers with

each roar as the

TV turns into

               static

      lightning

slashing a

smoldering tree limbs with

electricity willing

being out for

two days before

Noah's arc lit will eat

Jonah's lunch with these

wolves and lions

howling and roaring

passing two by four-ish

16.

tree's breach windows like

claws through the

glass as the

air roars louder through the

room

pelting drops in

lit by

      lightning

following

my eyes no longer

see through the

super soak as the

wind winds up and

pins me to

my knees

praying for an

olive branch

dove to bring

back the light

17.

closing in behind

me the door

slaps my ass

sideways against any wall

I think

I slide down to the

dampening carpet on

all fours

I find my

instinct as a

pouncing way

down the hall and

pawing the bath-

room door

open

curling up on the

sopping wet mat

18.

      tongue out panting

      flicking of the door

      back and forth with

      my make-

      shift snout and

      leap into the shower curtain

      paws first and

      roll onto my back to

      jab the drain

      plug and

      chop my head on the

      facet bleeding

      I let out a

      howling roaring

      pain

                    lightning

through

      my eyes

                   shaking

my body

19.

floating around in a

lit blood tinted water

I am a life

raft on the

ancient

aliens show

flying away

dripping into a

white whale

spooning around the

horn while pushing

greedily into a

used harpoon

estate sailor moon

20.

I wait in the shower as the

water rises up on the

floor

roaring

howling

surging air

pulls and

tears and

shreds the

curtains to

slap my back and

my hands covering

my head and

collapses into a

Jonah wail

21.

what about that

Bob Dylan

dream I had

go on

ask

he told me road rash

was the best way to

restore your faith in

your instincts and

balances life's

mysteries on a thin

thread as

long as

your heart is

lighter than a

matchstick

22.

wind swirls and

begins to

cry

slowly

softening

rain scatters and

subsides

I am on

my own two feet again

no longer in the

soak the

howls and

roars of

lions and wolves

storming thru

my bedroom

just like a human

who has to

deal with the waking

force of natural

light

23.

morning sun off the

dew threw the

fog off the

light of a

sun beam still

it's not a

rose a

pause a

waterfall in a

drought on the

phone app with a

headache raging and

clawing as

kittens with

puppy eyes

24.

again

poolside

mojitos

spill for the

seep divers and

history survivors

long live the

warning weather

birds of a

feather

dancers

prancers

one night

chancers

take it to the

deep end and

hold your breath

Rush

the

Light

I offer this while addressing posts on a green and yellow shiny day; sing

yourself into the vast purple and orange dreams while making

strides to feel the red and blues in your presence.

blink

the grit of the glaciers

the rise and falls of the Potomac

the silt and the settlement of the Thames

the wool around the Avon

the flint chips from the hills

all made my eyes the

bones and

muscles and

skin and

hair of

this human now

midway through

his life

to be in this place

changing the same as a

wish on the lips of

another

whistling

blown in the blink of an

eyelash

oral tradition

Detroit

poet and artist

I am a mine of salt of the

earth underneath us and

I import the iron that

manufactures the muscle that

drives the renewal of

our resources

I craft within my abilities

my creativity

ingenuity and work hard in

this furnace of sun and snow to

assemble these lines

hacking a futurist from Marinetti's muscle
car manifesto

I exalt

      his aggressive

      lifestyle as a

      feverish maniac

His racer stride

      is an Armstrong leap a

      fist pump and

      high five

He said and I echo the

      world's magnificence

      has a new beauty the

      beauty of speed

I want to be the

      man beyond the wheel

      who hurls his car across the

      Earth's express lanes on its orbit

Tesla's

light bouncing against the

current of electrons in the

every leaf of grass

ball spins into a

coil under the

right field corner

flashing in and out of the

shadows of the

night game lights

my body rounds second for a

chance to be a

dusting off a third bag

fireworks

Boom, Flash

                  Boom, BoOM, BOOM

        Flash Sprays Sizzle

my cigar lights the fuse

sparks flare and spit and smoke the

green fuse wires the

series of 500gm. cakes in

order to flower above the

branches from a tree and

expand into a sphere

comet tails

light the thunder above

our eyes and

reflects the stars and the

moon and the

 fireworks and

you

ex-pats

    1. Bacon on the Street

when I was living in London in 1992

you could buy Doc

Martens with Union Jack's

painted on them at a shop

called Sex on Carnaby Street in Soho

I am still very confused by this

I think the

boots were vegan friendly too

Francis Bacon hung out there and

got drunk all over the street

it was pretty good around

there for the most part 'til

someone set off a nail

bomb at a nightclub

Bloody Mess

then it was off to

Camden to work with the

Winehouse

OD.

ex-pats

    2. wild pictures on a gray day

strolling on a gray day through the

marble halls of

painted history as

3-D illusions of adorn

time and space

trapped it in a framed

conditioned still life

what is it about? the

Rokeby Venus

disproportionate sexuality that

reflexes in us the

charm and guile of the

female form with

its curves and colors

I sit and watch

what it is like to

live with the beauty and

scars of a feminist knife

slashing and gashing at a

hundred years ago

another man

painting frightened Eves to

reveal the phosphorescence of

death watching a

naked girl on a sofa

is paradise lost in its

biblical sense of fear and

longing in

I don't think

I am naïve enough to

call it innocence nor

am I that arrogant to

call it something wild or

primitive these urges to

confront life in

multiples and using maybe

there is something

frightening in the raw

young beauty that

makes us want to stay part of

it as long as we can in a

Self Portrait with Hat

docile gray days inside

these marble halls

there is no bare

space on the walls

where a painting of a

decaying corpse of a

still living man should be

just a living man

observing how close

I am to immortality

I know we are all

damaged before we die

only the illusions

outlive and

stay this still

ex-pats

    3.   Stoker's garden

we'd take the train from Thorpe

Surrey down the Thames to

Waterloo and

ride the Underground to

Piccadilly Circus

out we'd walk

dodging people like arrows from

Cupid's bow into the

Lair of the

White Worm tequila shots

we drank laybacks and

rode saddled bar stools

others drank straight from the

pitcher or

double shots of

Wild Jack

we filled the bar with

smoke and laughter

hoping for no discipline

some fought in alleys with the

Death Doom of the

Double Born

others threw up in piss or

sucked a dick while

we waited for

taped hockey games inside a

Maple Leaf

we'd walk out into the

daylight like

knights or cowgirls to

watch the Punch and Judy

turn Jewels into

Seven Stars a day

I hesitant to call it

Andrew Lloyd Webber's town though

his name Shrouds

every marque around

I know I felt safer in

Stoker's Garden

we'd march into

Dracula's breath before the

last train

passing the Haagen Dazs and

Hippodrome and

arguing with the soapbox

apocalypse about context

that every year's end

is a new beginning

we'd push and pull

each other back Underground with

minds and gaps and

trains

we'd heap into the car where the

Man from Texas

started to sing the

stars and stripes into

two fisted locals as

red glares led to

accusations of IRA

I explained that this

our time in London

is an education

not a suicide attempt to

filled cars with the

sound of American

Pie and cigarettes and

goodbyes that cleared the

stale smoke from

station to station 'til

we were home again

later that year

back channel the moon

maybe we can work

something out

something alongside these

hills

vines and

glowing orange bonfire pits

deep red grapes cast their claim from the

air

whether it is an instant or a

book the

green leaves turn in the wind to

shift our shadows

you

you look through your phone to

other places

distant to me

me

I look at the red sunset through the

clouds to

grow and ripen

or

is it that the white moon?

shifting that which binds

us to our currents and tidings

you hold the back of my bold hair and

almost kick over the

yellow wine bottle on the

glass coffee table as

it settles

your legs keep twitching

I rise up and grab the

green wine bottle and

drink in red bliss

you slide a smirk sideways as

I toss you a towel with

your tan belly all scrunched up from the

fold of the couch

I take another swig of

red wine and wink

you bite your lip and

blink your eyes

slowly while wiggling your hips

I turn and glide through the

open sliding door

light a cigarette

"yes

I see you Moon"

I wink and

wash down the earthy vine

washes over the red-hot bonfire of

my harvesting heart

big grin

Sailing the blue stream through

treee ee blowing

telling the green timberland

floating to remind me of an

island

two of us flee the fleet to

red sun streets with

blue ribbons in your hair

astute and flowing

stripping the time away

not here

not now

red streaming live on

your tablet

seeing into the blue eyes of

forever this kind of

present tensions

speaking of the violent in the

time of the violent and

explosions and experience and

remembering before the

war's last break was

breaking the sidewalks in two

how to pay for yesterday?

night before the

yellow stream of cocktails the

apostate leaves a pontiff

still soaring in that hat

I know I will move you

telling you more and store the

distant dialogue of

now and a

core bold stance

another dance

I love that dance

another yellow drink and

stance jawing life into a

tipster up to the

moon

soon I will see the

skin your dress

doesn't share with the

rest of the room

back and forth alone under

your shoulder blades

another yellow drink

fizzes stunning

my height and

wait

I float upon

your laughing

holding onto the

ceiling feeling

theatre from London

first time I saw the
Rocky Horror Picture Show
I thought it was weird to
see the Butler from
Clue in lingerie

following the week
I saw Eraserhead and then
went to see the staged
production of Rocky Horror

what a wild and
lacy train ride

I wore brown boots
blue jeans and
purple and
green plaid flannel shirt a
forest green waxed jacket with a
hood hanging off the back and a

green Sparty baseball

cap backwards

half drunk

I did the time warp again

cowgirl up

outside on

slabs of grey concrete meeting
I am told to be grateful for
each and every one under me for
this Earth is in
constant emotion in a
solar system that is just one in a
galaxy that is just one in a
universe still expanding after
its singularity creation of
than itself

worrying as
I am rooting
desiring the divine display and
deserving the divine presence
this is your laughter and the
longing to be a blackhole

500g. cakes

4th of July at
night on Rosa Parks Blvd
we spent the day behind the row houses
matching up 500gm cakes with
rows of 3" shells on the flattest pieces of
warped particle board

I pull out a long green coil of fuse from a
clear plastic bag and uncoil it
we cut it into foot long fuses
I pinch a part a pack of twist ties and
begin the work of connecting the
 shortened coils to the small
fuses in the base of each cake

we couple together each fuse to the
other cakes and stage our show in
five acts on five
separate particle boards

noon sun starts to fall above us as the

sweat drips down from our foreheads

now there is a party starting to gather

it is time to fire up the grill

turn on the DJ's booth and

dance and feast 'til the sun begins to

give way to our sparkle streamers crackling

quickening bursting star's into strobes

Toulouse-Lautrec

found it easy to

draw a horse

growing up in the countryside

art school in Paris thought so

does da Vinci?

he was a military advisor in Milan

who couldn't cast a horse statue

due to the lack of

bronze cannons for the city's defense

is there something molten in?

Henri's work

pastel crayon scraps and a

troubadour's poster melts in the

rain to rinse away the life

he would never live up to in Montmartre

brush stroke paints a

red windmill to

flash the white fluff of a

black stocking leg kick

not many can travel to Europe inside the

aluminum body of a plane

leave alone in a steam liner

even if we aren't buried

next to a nun

we will see his drawings and

paintings and

outlive the symphysis beyond

his 36 years

I dreamt about Dali St. Petes and Chris in
Columbus cannibalizing my tears

white brakeman's handkerchief

unfolding from the back

pocket into a blanket

wool vest (orange to blue)

I wiped my eyes 'til

they bleed virgin's blood and

breathe gas from a

crack in the Earth's core

molten drops of red pumice

ripped my black lungs into a

blue and orange

stained glass oven

my arms erupt into buttresses

flying across the Earth's surface

my legs cross over

my grape leaf groin with a

gift shop full of souvenirs

selling white candle wax and

wicks for the unforgiven

grasp of chance

then a lance causes the pour of the

wine into my heart

fluttering through the filters of

my skin rising from the

yeast in the air dipped in the

olive branch and

dried salt tears and soaked in the

bread dough and placed back into

my yellow and purple stained

glass ribcage vaulted oven for an

hour and fifteen minutes

it wasn't sacrilege to dream this

it was a masking effort to

live off the steam in my tears

Omaha, Normandy

sometimes
I walk to the edge and bluff
sometimes
I walk to the edge and it the
water licks my toes cold

these dunes are held together with
green dune grass between
white crosses over sandy beaches
where the wild boar's trace
paths between fences

I was not old enough to drive but
I was old enough to drink
I was young
I was young and
I shall never drink again(sic)

Caen is not known for its wine
more for its conquests than the

finger bone of a saint

Michelle's Monts is
better than the tide
you can always go to the edge
when the tide is out

remember
that shithole in the ground
is a unisex toilet and the
digestif still burns a
hole through the roof of
my heart

Sunflowers

mating pair of
goldfinch's land on the
highest bloom of the
sunflowers

they pluck the burnt
orange petals off
one by one with
their beaks and
peck to clean the
seeds and swallow

now
they are not a pair the
yellow one will fly in on
his wave and chirps
then feasts

then the
green one will

pop up for a quick

snack and squawk

this time though

I try to approach

them together as they

peck and pluck a mess of

seeds and chirps

just for a sec or so

they don't notice and

don't care

how close I am to them

again the

yellow one

leaps off top and flaps away

quick to flee the

green one blinks then

flutters a follow

Clandestine in Grey

clad in a black

t-shirts and blue jeans

I help bring in the water bottles

I help bring in the white table clothes and

white plastic silverware rolled in

white napkins tied with red ribbons

advertisers bring us the

local brew keg the

pop and wine with trays of

vegetables and

fruits and

sandwiches

fabulous ruins of Detroit's decay porn

projector sets up in the unfinished bar

while mics

drums

guitars

amps

turntables

load onto the stage as

paintings and sculptors

fill up the entry hall

they tell me how

excited they are for

being a part of our 'zine launch the

furnace Detroit

I am already tired from the

build up and stuffing packets

full of other people's fliers and

my 'zine as I shake

their hands and smile back

outside the

owner of the hall

made a deal with the

local drug dealers to

not bother the party goer's cars

that are starting to

line the streets of the

mostly abandoned

neighborhood

line at the door

wraps around the cars in the

gravel parking lot

$10 a head and

they carry a packet

around all night or

they leave it

all over the floor

food is devoured and to

begin the dancing

later that night the

'Rave' squad

shows up in urban grey

assault fatigues carrying their

shiny steel shotguns with

black Maglite attached and lit

lit in our faces

fair amount of partiers

pour down the stairs and

flow out the doors

I tell them to stay and

it will be ok but

they don't hesitate to

stop and listen

so it couldn't be a

few minutes later the

'Rave' squad

re-appears with

their heads down and

I say thanks for scarring off the

patrons of

our charity event and

they don't even stop to listen as

they leave in a huff

you see the

City Council and the

local State Legislators

were there with the Press

so it couldn't be a 'Rave' and

I walk back upstairs and

apologize to them

they know it was not

my fault and

I usher them into

our 'VIP' room

office space for

drinks and a few games of pool

while the beats still

pump on for the brave and the

don't give a fucks

old vine zen

       1.   color wheel (paints)

blue shade

splays across

my windshield and

my dashboard over

my color wheel

yellow sunlight taps into

my eyes off the

mirror windows of the

RenCen's cylinders

I drive along the straight river down

Jefferson the

red bottle of wine pings off the

metal rails under

my seat as

I break for

traffic lights at

tunnel on-ramp

I cruise up the flow of the
river with the
traffic from
downtown born ready to
hum along with the radio
windows down

I hear the cars and trucks
flux back and forth on
both sides of my ride while
other stereos
pulse and pull into mine

another green light slows a
series of bottle clanks so
I reach my hand back behind
my seat and
grab the green
bottle from underneath it

I grip it sideways on the

passenger seat the

purple liquid looks up at me and

winks

I let it go to

slide back and forth and

settle down shotgun

I stop at a bar with

prohibition posters on the walls and

post-punk songs on the jukebox and

drink craft beer with an orange slice and

sit on an old church pew that

bends a moans and crackles underneath me

one beer

becomes two beers and then

I move on from the

park and drive the

purple bottle bouncing from the

back of the passenger side to the

floor as

I shift up through the gears

left turn then
right into the neighborhood
streets back and forth from the
stop signs and
green lights 'til
I pull up the drive of
her mother's home

unlatching the gate
I walk into the backyard and
wave to her mother in
her yellow and red sunroom and
continue into the blue
carriage house in the backyard

she is still not home from the
horse farm riding camp where
she works as an instructor and
I realize I forgot the
Zin in my car

she sends me a text while
I warm up the couch with a
cold beer and a
comedy show

I text her back
she's ready for home a
shower and the wine
still in my ride

old vine zen

    2. primary (strokes)

red sun

yellow leaf

blue flower

priming all the colors

I canvas the scene

stretching out for me

blue screen

yellow stem

blossoms into

red blooms

drawing on vellum

bleached by the sun above

my Exact-o knife blade

cuts through to the self

healing skin of vinyl that

never really heals

just leaves thin scars from

each cut that

shapes the flowers

I float them between

two pieces of glass the

flowers' shadow creates a

3-D space behind it like

living flowers above a

vase

old vine zen

    3.   secondary (canvas)

we are

still wet from

our shower together

green bottle pops

open from the pressure I apply to the

screwed in dumb waiter

I unwind the orange cork from the

screw and smell it

just for fun

naked

you bring me your glass and

kiss me hard and slow as

I fill it near over flow with the

purple Zin

you spin around to the TV remote and

turn it on while grabbing the

Chicago DVD I bought you and

lay it gently into the player

you retracted the musical as

you press play and

fast forward to

your favorite scene

you stop and

press play and

begin to dance like Zeta-Jones

your hands move from hips to tits as

I taste the air and wine of

our new vine

Color Theory

bends (knots)

cut the

bends begin to

repair the braids of

two equal lengths

not distant

just frayed

each turn

brings a closeness

not whole

stained blood red and

sky blue

rainbow oil and

salted strain

rope burns and

heals what the knots can't conceal

luchadores

it is night again on the Rosa's Blvd
we reveal the particle boards
covered by our fused-up offerings

we wear our luchador masks
found packaged in an offering and
pray our way through the gathering masses

amen rises above our
"bless you" and "hell no's" as
we make it to the street corner

we set up each particle board in
order for our congregation across the
mouth of Leverette St

one of us is an alcoholic the
other is an emerging mad man
together
we are pyro preaching wrestlers

we shed our colorful masks

mount halo flashlights to our foreheads

this year is another Alpha and

Omega show above our lives

missionary possible

tide

sand from the dunes

is a fire hot coals under your toes?

warm salt on your skin a

deep blue after a

cool wave swim

sea shore howls in through your eyes a

water mists and shards of quartz sift

more salt and

suntan lotion and

foam and

dirt and

shells and

stone and

sun shining

spraying into the

revolving shoreline

is it so much to

view the rise of a wave

pushing up out of the ocean in

foams and fizz

it is bliss beyond the delicate nature of

beast and

bird and

burden baring a simple

look into survival

nonage

I'm shattering
beer bottles with
butterflies into
parachuting plastic men before the
sunset before the
roman candles light off the
rocket's red glaze

I've hid in the grey dust gravel pits
armed with a brown glass bottle
loaded with blue rockets and
ambushed my cousin and brother with a
sizzling
whistling
near hit repeated as
he was readying his reply in an
echoing report

die a pause

she tells me
she's from the Phoenix red
somewhere along the Atlantic grey or
was it Mediterranean blue

I tell her
I saw a movie awhile ago with a
green
yellow
purple tattoo of a
speckled hen or was it a trout while
she glimpses at my buttons
fly on the rise

she tells me
she works in hot topics and
I ask her about
all of the wrong ones

I tell her

I really don't want to

talk politics that

go soo good with beer

she tells me

her new lover

loves the silver chains

I bought her

I tell her

I'm glad there

are no policies for this

Easter egg mass

she tells me

she likes that

I have made the

effort to affect her

I tell her

I will die before her and

she hands me a daisy

full of lead bb's

combustible

sugar skull red star
magnet fixed to the hatchback
identifies the speed in
which I have passed the
expressway traffic
now behind me

I raise my foot off the
gas pedal slightly and
watch the digital gauge for the
mpg on the dash
skip around from 5.0 to 36.3 to
26.4 to 42.0 to 12.6
paces my car
out of their view

phosphenes

while I have suffered
life's stings and narrow misses
I have been to a
few fantastic parties
like the one I was at
last night

we left before the
cops showed up
it was much later
than I thought a
friend of mine
freaked out under the
intense thumping of the
sound system and the
blue and white
lasers beaming and bouncing off the
black trash bags on the
wall and ceiling
mixing well with the cartoon

faces on the paper tabs

I talked her

down in my car

down the street from the

abandoned tan

brick strip mall

we tried to re-

enter the party but the

bouncer wanted to

charge us the cover

again

so we left

I drove her home

since I had work

today on the west side

I left her at her red brick

apartment in the sunrise and

rode on down the

expressway with fluffy white

pollen floating in the

brightening sunlight

I rubbed my eyes to

watch the yellow glitter

sparkle around the memory of

her glowing sunset eyes

I still have yet to

slept under these

stale bright neon fixtures at

work in the stock room

cloud chamber

fog rolls the

mist sticks above the

rolling river over

rocks pool and spills

      down falls

ripples white foam and spray

carving a deeper pool reflecting the

      clouds

racing across the blue sky

      atmosphere below the

brown and black

white capped mountains

yellow sun

              blinks

behind the cloud chamber as the

      river bubbles and

cascades further

down the rocky tree line

      slope

fireworks 2

our fireworks aren't

exactly illegal but

they aren't as original as sin

now that I think of it

they weren't mentioned in the

ten commandments

I always thought

they're more of a

sign a

burning bush or

even a celebration of the

Earth and the sky

aligning themselves in an

optical solution

henge

campfire spits and crackles

steam and smoke off the

top of the flame's reach

small stones circle the ash and the

amber glow of the

burning logs and twigs

stacking up crisscross with

plenty of space to

allow the fire to

breath and light up the

faces of its creators to

feed them its heat and

dance the flicker into

their eyes

Helios

solar flares
molten white overheating
his own idea of self
lashing out at his magnetism for the
system of elliptical orbits

we still haven't decided
how many planets he has but
he surrounds us with his belt

other heavenly bodies
wobble and spin with
their own moons to worry about

some superstitions believe
they are the old gods and
wish they had more influence

Helios has the mass to
pull them around and they orbit him in

their ellipses as they have for millennia

there are few that
could have been true stars but
are now colder than our poles

though we are lucky to have the
blue and green Earth we have
she knows we've outgrown
most of her temper and comforts yet
she tries and bothers

miles away from us
Helios is slow to burn
orange to red and
devour us and
never let us implode

Icarus' brew pub

I ride a reliance on
liquid currents and the
taste of its uplifting foam

my hands are wings of
molded aluminum on an
anti-gravity stool

I leave this ground to
hit bull's eyes to
tenderize their rib eyes

roaring one

tonight at the
show reading
I drink a Pinot from the
rushing
river valley of the
San Pedro bookstore
held hostage within the
poet's breath

cork smells
like salty sand and
cigarette smoke tells no
lies about flammability of
oxygen tanks
drunk tanks
think tanks

do you like it really?
is it me to let? the
light rush in

it would rage

blind and bind to a

rock and

birth from a thigh and

steal from the sun and

teach the stars

our myths for their science

I hold my wine glass to

my ear and listen to the

top and hear the

clapture's and wonder if

there has been enough neglect to

grow in this gravel spit and

sandy sail drought and

I sip

I am not as strong as

this pouring from the

roaring one

spoiling for the blood of a

disassembled poet

line from limb

light starts to blur and

stings my eyes still

I look through the

legs of my glass of

Noir upstage to the

crowded applause

eight ball in the side

I ride the bus back

home from Stratford after

running a table at a

pub just younger

than Shakespeare

I exit the bus at

Wooton Wawen and walk and

pass the caravans at the Hall as

I head up to Badger's Hill to

our home in Preston Bagot

my fingers hesitate on

my phone as I try to

rise above the Spitfire valley with the

kisses and English playing

soft and hard over the

green grass soil under the

soles of my well-worn shoes

sawbones says

drink more electricity

fortify your tolerance for
decay and decadence

remember to linger still in the
stars and refill
your memories of
birthday parties and
cheesecake panty
subscriptions in
commando fatigues
while patronizing the law with
prayers in an
enveloped click

Julio Cortazar's "To be Read in the Interrogative" (to be read as a Jack Spicer imitation)

Have you seen

Have you truly seen

the snow, the stars, the plush

                  steps of the breeze

Have you touched

Have you really touched

the plate, the bread, the face of

                  the woman you loved

                  so much

Have you lived with

this blow to the forehead

the instant, the painting, the fall

                  the blood

Have you known in

every pore of your skin, known

how your eyes, your hands, your gender

                        your limp heart

had to be thrown

had to be mourned

had to invent another self

a flight not All Ways

Well, here's to your independence
blue skies back the grey clouds of
your flight. The air under the
balcony slips through your lift
down to the black top road.

I wish your happiness
and survival. It is
yours now, the
air, the grey
white over
the black
top.

the Epitaph

is an extracting erasuresque
conversation between Anne Waldman's
intro. to The Scripture of the Golden
Eternity by Jack Kerouac and Jack
Kerouac's The Scripture of the Golden
Eternity as a quote for
NYE.

"When you've understood this
scripture, throw it away. If
you can't understand this
scripture, throw it away. I
insist on your freedom."

Anne:

in the midst of their energetic

comradeship meaning to sew a

thread or yarn it carries the

orally delivered record of

canons in the figure of Coyotes as

meticulous wit these illogical

syllogisms sound like gibberish

they're golden to a poet's ear in

which the mind may tell disparate

without my soaring dreams to take

place in a perfectly silent mind

this topsy-turvy logic quite

naturally riffing on this conundrum

quite a bit deified notion of

existence as well as through my

nihilistic interpretation of life

We're all just conglomerations of

tendencies hopeless bundles of

quivering meat bound on a wheel of

cuts sleeping (the wheel for suffering

existence) deceptively simple vigorous

lanes to frolic from a spell

apparently for about sixty seconds

golden in the sun's eyelids

eternity vivid and generous and

timeless hipster scriptorium into the

Void!

Jack:

Did I create that sky? That is why
I am the golden eternity. The cure of the
world's woe is a beat stick. each
note a shrine fantastic magic
imaginations of the lightning, flash,
plays, dreams not even plays, dreams in the
thunderbolt received of the
endless offering of her dark void.
Blind milky light fills overnights and
morning is a crystal. The
world was spun of a blade of
grass! eternity milky love, the
white light everywhere everything
shining and awake, cats sleep.
The everlasting and tranquil essence,
said the Coyote to the earthmaker the
butterfly doesn't take it as a
personal achievement, humble and not-
even-here, Cats yawn because
they realize that there's nothing to

do. The puma's tourist face continuous to

look at the blue sky with sightless

eyes, verdurous paradise planted in mid

air! at

night under the moon

www.ingramcontent.com/pod-product-compliance
Lightning Source LLC
Chambersburg PA
CBHW070529090426
42735CB00013B/2911